Most Outrageous Outlaws

Trish Hurley

Series Editor
Jeffrey D. Wilhelm

Much thought, debate, and research went into choosing and ranking the 10 items in each book in this series. We realize that everyone has his or her own opinion of what is most significant, revolutionary, amazing, deadly, and so on. As you read, you may agree with our choices, or you may be surprised — and that's the way it should be!

Franklin Watts®

an imprint of

SCHOLASTIC

www.scholastic.com/librarypublishing

A Rubicon book published in association with Scholastic Inc.

Rubicon © 2008 Rubicon Publishing Inc.
www.rubiconpublishing.com

Associate Publishers: Kim Koh, Miriam Bardswich
Project Editor: Amy Land
Editor: Elizabeth Siegel
Creative Director: Jennifer Drew
Project Manager/Designer: Jeanette MacLean
Graphic Designer: Sherwin Flores

The publisher gratefully acknowledges the following for permission to reprint copyrighted material in this book.

Every reasonable effort has been made to trace the owners of copyrighted material and to make due acknowledgment. Any errors or omissions drawn to our attention will be gladly rectified in future editions.

"Law Officer's Widow Upset Over Fame of Bonnie and Clyde" (excerpt) by Bud Kennedy. From the *Forth Worth Star-Telegram*, June 1, 1996. Reprinted with permission.

Cover image: Jesse James–Library of Congress; All other images–istockphoto

Library and Archives Canada Cataloguing in Publication

Hurley, Trish
    The 10 most outrageous outlaws / Trish Hurley.

Includes index.
ISBN: 978-1-55448-506-2

    1. Readers (Elementary). 2. Readers—Outlaws.
I. Title. II. Title: Ten most outrageous outlaws.

PE1117.H874 2007   428.6   C2007-906930-4

1 2 3 4 5 6 7 8 9 10   10   17 16 15 14 13 12 11 10 09 08

Printed in Singapore

Contents

6

18

38

WANTED:
DEAD OR ALIVE!

Outlaw. Gunslinger. Gangster. What do these words make you think of? Ruthless criminals who should be severely punished? Or Robin Hood types of bandits who robbed the rich to help the poor?

The second half of the 19th century was downright dangerous in North America. The West was being opened rapidly and law enforcement was definitely not the organized system the United States has today. That's why most people think of outlaws as gun-toting bandits running wild across the Wild West.

There were opportunities for outlaws in the early 20th century, too. In 1929, an economic crisis called the Great Depression began. It left millions of people jobless as banks, farms, and factories were forced to close. At this time, the manufacture and distribution of alcohol was illegal due to Prohibition, a law that lasted until 1933. The pressures of the Great Depression and the opportunities of illegal liquor sales encouraged many people into a life of crime.

In these turbulent years, the poor often felt that wealthy bankers and landowners did not treat them fairly. As a result, when outlaws robbed stagecoaches, trains, and banks, people sometimes sympathized with them. Some outlaws became folk heroes, with songs and outlandish tales written about them!

Several of these outlaws have become legendary. Yet nothing can change the fact that they were criminals and sometimes murderers. As we considered who to put on our list of outrageous outlaws, we asked ourselves: How dangerous were these men and women? How long were they outlaws? How wild were their reputations? As you read these outlaws' amazing stories, ask yourself:

---

turbulent: *marked by disorder and disturbance*
outlandish: *strange; fantastic*

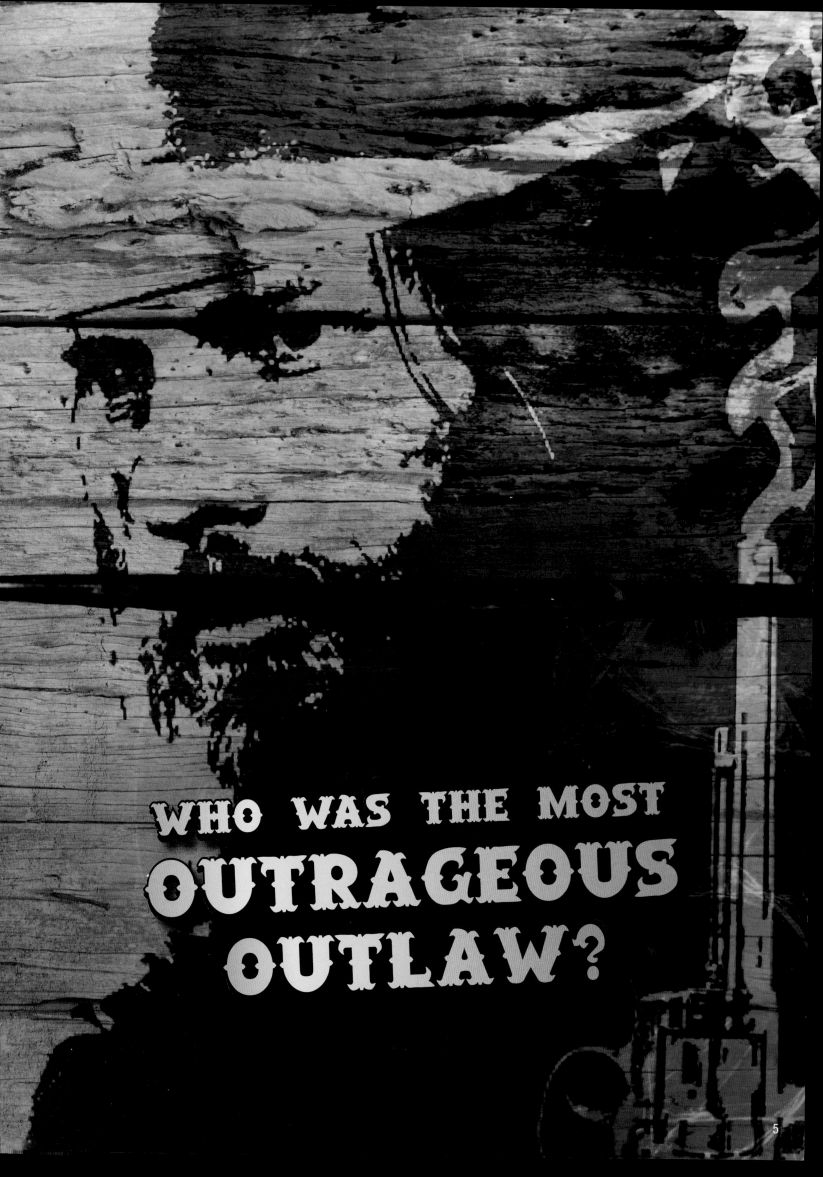

WHO WAS THE MOST
OUTRAGEOUS
OUTLAW?

10 BELLE STARR

*A portrait of Belle Starr in 1870 —
was her reputation as a gunslinging
outlaw fact or fiction?*

REAL NAME: Myra Maybelle Shirley

ALSO KNOWN AS: Belle Starr and the Bandit Queen

ERA: 1868 to 1889

BEST KNOWN FOR: Rivaling any male gunslinger in the Wild West as a rootin', tootin', shootin' outlaw

Belle Starr captured the American public's imagination by being in the company of famous outlaws like Jesse James and the Younger brothers. But was she really the outrageous outlaw that people believed her to be?

Starr was raised in a wealthy household. She was exposed to outlaws from a young age when gang members hid out in her family home. Drawn to their lifestyle, Starr married Jim Reed in 1866, a man whose murderous ways would set them on the run from the law.

Rumors abound about Starr's participation in robberies and bootlegging. No one knows for sure how many of the countless stories about her are true, but many tales paint her as a real criminal mastermind, and establish Belle Star as a true American outlaw.

---

bootlegging: *illegal production, distribution, and sale of alcohol*

BELLE STARR

BACKGROUND

Starr was born in Missouri in 1848. She was the only daughter out of six children. By the 1860s, her family owned several businesses and was wealthy enough to send Starr to private school. During the Civil War, the family moved to Texas where they became friendly with the Younger brothers and a number of other outlaws.

MOST OUTRAGEOUS CRIMES

The only crime that Starr was ever convicted of was horse theft. In 1882, she and her second husband, Sam Starr, were working on a farm and stealing horses on the side. They used the farmer's corral to store their stolen horses, but the jig was up when the farmer noticed that some of the horses looked a lot like those of his neighbors. Starr and her husband were convicted, and they served nine months of a one-year sentence.

The Expert Says...

" Though she was raised to be 'ladylike' by her ... wealthy parents, Belle Starr was born to be a rebel. Although she had big brown eyes and dark hair, Belle was described as 'hatchet-faced' and mean as a rattlesnake. "

— Katherine Krohn, author of *Women of the Wild West*

Quick Fact

Starr had two children with her first husband. Her daughter Pearl also went on to become a famous outlaw. Ed, her youngest child, spent time in jail for horse theft, but later became a police officer.

IN THE END

Starr's second husband was killed in a gunfight in 1886. She continued to help other outlaws until 1889, when she was shot in the back and killed. There were no witnesses and the identity of her killer remains a mystery.

Quick Fact

A book called *Bella Starr, the Bandit Queen, or the Female Jesse James* was published the year of Starr's death. It was sold as a biography, but was filled with wild stories that helped turn Belle Starr into a legend.

? Why do you think a publisher would print a biography that was known to be factually incorrect?

10

8   7   6

WHODUNIT?

THE EVENTS

Starr and Jim July, her last husband, spent the night with friends. The next day, July went to Fort Smith to face charges of horse stealing, and Starr headed home.

On her way, she stopped to visit her neighbors. After leaving their house, Starr rode into an ambush. She was knocked out of her saddle and killed by two gunshots.

THE SUSPECTS

EDGAR A. WATSON

Starr's tenant, a farmer who rented land from Starr. Watson was angry with Starr. She had forced him to leave after finding out he was wanted by the police on charges of murder.

Watson was at the neighbors' house at the same time as Starr, but had left just before her. Starr had to ride past Watson's house to get home, and investigators found a trail leading from the ambush site to a spot near Watson's home.

PEARL REED

Starr's daughter. Starr had broken up Pearl's engagement and Pearl was furious about it. Their relationship was also strained because at one point, Starr had driven a pregnant Pearl out of their home.

ED REED

Starr's son. Apparently Ed didn't like his mother's relationship with Jim July. Starr had also whipped Ed on several occasions, and Ed had been overheard threatening Starr about her harsh discipline.

JIM JULY

Starr's last husband. His life with Starr had been unhappy for some time. Did he really go to Fort Smith? Or was he waiting to ambush and kill her?

Take Note

There's no question that Belle Starr's behavior was outrageous for a woman in the Wild West. Although she was convicted of horse theft, it was never proven that she committed the countless crimes reported in newspapers and books. Nevertheless, the Bandit Queen's unconventional behavior and wild reputation help her gallop into the #10 spot on our list.
• Do you think an outlaw's ranking on our list should be based on actual deeds, reputation, or a combination of both?

5 4 3 2

Many people who met Black Bart were taken in by his polite and charming personality.

REAL NAME: Charles E. Bowles

ALSO KNOWN AS: Black Bart, Charles E. Bolton, and T. Z. Spalding

ERA: 1875 to 1883

BEST KNOWN FOR: Robbing stagecoaches and writing poetry!

Some say Black Bart was the most unusual outlaw in the history of the Wild West. His criminal "career" didn't begin until he was in his forties — then he went wild. He robbed over 28 stagecoaches in just eight years. During these robberies, he never once fired his gun. In fact, some historians say he didn't even load it. He was also known for being polite and twice he left poems behind at the scenes of his crimes!

Black Bart started off life as Charles E. Bowles. (He later changed his last name to Boles.) When he was 20, he went to California to try gold mining. In 1854, he married Mary Elizabeth Johnson. They lived on a farm and had four children. When the Civil War broke out, Bowles fought on the Union side for three years. Upon his discharge, he went back to farming but soon lost interest. So he went to seek his fortune in mining.

Bowles found a mine in Montana and began working it himself. Some men from the Wells Fargo bank offered to buy the mine. When Bowles refused, they cut off his water supply. Bowles had no choice but to give up the mine. Eventually he stopped writing letters home and his family assumed he had died. He wasn't dead, but the outlaw Black Bart (as Bowles called himself) was born. In 1875, Black Bart robbed the first of many Wells Fargo stagecoaches. It was the beginning of an outrageous outlaw's life of crime.

---

stagecoaches: *horse-drawn carriages that carried passengers, parcels, and mail*

discharge: *release from military duty*

 Do you think losing his mine to Wells Fargo drove Bowles to a life of crime? Why or why not?

BLACK BART

BACKGROUND

Charles E. Bowles was born in Norfolk County, England, in 1829. When he was two, he moved to upstate New York with his family. He grew up on a farm there and attended the local public school where he excelled in sports.

MOST OUTRAGEOUS CRIMES

On July 26, 1875, Black Bart stopped a Wells Fargo stagecoach in Calavaras County, California, by pointing a shotgun at the driver. The bandit's head was covered with a flour sack with two eyeholes cut out. He told the driver to throw down the money box. Then he called out, "If he dares shoot, give him a solid volley, boys." The driver noticed several rifles aimed at him from behind some boulders, so he threw down the box and drove away. Later, when the driver returned to the scene, he saw the "rifles" were still there. Upon further inspection, he realized they were actually sticks wedged in the rocks.

volley: *firing a number of rifles at the same time*

IN THE END

Wells Fargo detectives finally tracked down Black Bart in 1883. He agreed to return some of his buried loot if he was charged with only one robbery. Black Bart was sentenced to six years in jail, but was let out after four years for good behavior. Soon after he was released, he disappeared and was never heard from again.

Quick Fact

Guess how the detectives found Black Bart? They traced a laundry tag on a handkerchief that Black Bart had accidentally left behind during one of his robberies.

The Expert Says...

" [Black Bart is] ... a person of great endurance. Exhibited genuine wit under most trying circumstances. Extremely proper and polite in behavior, eschews profanity. "

— Harry N. Morse, one of the detectives who caught Black Bart in 1883

eschews: *avoids, especially for moral reasons*

10   9   8   7   6

ARROGANT OR ARTISTIC?

Bowles gave himself the nickname "Black Bart." It's thought that he got the name from an outlaw character in a serial novel called *The Case of Summerfield*. In it, the robber was described as an "unruly and wild villain." Bowles might have thought that the name would help scare stagecoach drivers into giving him their money.

The public first became aware of Black Bart's name when he left a poem after his fourth robbery. He signed the poem Black Bart the PO8 (po-eight, as in poet).

Black Bart also left a poem after his fifth robbery. It read:

Black Bart

Here I lay me down to sleep
To wait the coming *morrow*,
Perhaps success, perhaps defeat
And everlasting sorrow.
Yet come what will, I'll try it once,
My conditions can't be worse,
And if there's money in that box,
'Tis money in my purse.

— Black Bart, the PO8

morrow: morning; next day

Quick Fact

After Black Bart was released from prison, a Wells Fargo stagecoach was robbed by a bandit who left behind a poem. But since the handwriting on that poem didn't match that on Black Bart's other two poems, it was assumed that the robber was a copycat.

Quick Fact

Some people believe that Black Bart disappeared in 1888 because Wells Fargo paid him to go away.

Take Note

Black Bart comes in at #9. He robbed many stagecoaches by relying on his wits. He never fired his gun and never robbed the passengers on the stagecoach. Some might say he was almost likeable!
• Do you think Black Bart would like holding the #9 ranking on our list? Do you think he would want to be ranked higher? On what kind of list might Black Bart make the #1 spot?

5   4   3   2   1

Bill Miner committed robberies in the United States and in Canada.

REAL NAME: It's a mystery! Some think he was born Ezra Allen Miner. Others think his birth name may have been McDonald.

ALSO KNOWN AS: Gentleman Bandit and the Gray Fox, and George Edwards when he moved to Canada

ERA: 1869 to 1911

BEST KNOWN FOR: Robbing stagecoaches and trains; breaking out of jail

Meet the man who is said to have first used the phrase: "HANDS UP!" Despite this claim to fame, Bill Miner is said to have been a gentleman. In fact, as he moved from community to community, he often had quite a number of admirers and friends. There was just one problem — Miner was a compulsive robber.

His fatal flaw seemed to be that he never learned his lesson. Miner's life was like a revolving door. Most of his time was spent holding up stagecoaches and trains, running from the law, getting caught, and then escaping from jail so that he could commit more robberies. His crime sprees were mainly centered in the United States, but when the police were getting close, he moved to Canada. There he committed the country's first train robbery. He later committed what was probably the least successful train robbery in Canada's history.

---

compulsive: *unable to resist*

BILL MINER

BACKGROUND

According to some sources, Ezra Allen Miner (later Bill Miner) was born in 1846 in Onondaga, Michigan. Miner's father died when he was a young boy. Miner and his mother then moved to a gold-mining town in California. He went to work earning low wages as a young miner. In 1864, Miner enlisted in the Union Army as a private. Less than three months later, he deserted the army and turned to crime.

private: *soldier of the lowest rank*

? What do you think are some of the factors that lead a young person like Bill Miner to a life of crime? What can society do to prevent this from happening?

MOST OUTRAGEOUS CRIMES

Bill Miner is best known for committing Canada's first train robbery in 1904. His first train robbery was a success, but his second attempt was definitely not! Miner and his gang targeted a Canadian Pacific Railway train on its way to Vancouver. But they mistakenly hit the baggage car instead of the express car (where the money was stored). By the time Miner realized his mistake, it was too late. He had already ordered the engineer to unhook the baggage car and drive away with the rest of the train. Miner netted $15 from the robbery and was captured a few days later.

IN THE END

Miner was jailed for robbing a train in Georgia in 1911. A few months later, he escaped. A posse caught him after 17 days. Then in June of 1912, Miner escaped again. He somehow managed to saw through both his prison chains and the bars on his window! After spending three days in a Georgia swamp, he was recaptured. Miner told the prison guards, "I guess I'm getting too old for this sort of thing." He died in prison on September 2, 1913.

posse: *temporary group of civilians who help with law enforcement*

Quick Fact

The public saw Bill Miner as a nice, gentlemanly criminal. When he died, a Sunday school teacher paid for his funeral so the outlaw could have a proper send-off!

The Expert Says...

" With his easygoing manner and love of children, he became an immediate favorite with young and old. No one who met the gray-haired Edwards (Bill Miner), with his stiff moustache and commanding eyes, either disliked or forgot him. For, even at the age of 60, Miner cut a striking figure. "

— T. W. Paterson, author of *Outlaws of Western Canada*

THE FIRST CANADIAN TRAIN ROBBERY

8

Bill Miner became famous for committing the first train robbery in Canada. Read about his outrageous crime in this article.

Quick Fact

Bill Miner started his criminal career robbing stagecoaches. During one of his long stints in jail, stagecoaches became obsolete. So when he got out of jail, he started robbing trains.

It happened around 9:30 P.M. on September 10, 1904. The Canadian Pacific Railway Express No. 1 was headed for Vancouver. It was loaded with gold dust from a goldmine in Ashcroft, British Columbia.

Along the way, three men snuck on board the train. Their leader was Bill Miner. The robbers headed for the express car where all the valuables were guarded. They threatened to use dynamite if the door to the car wasn't opened. Inside, they forced the express messenger to open the safe. The bandits escaped with $6,000 in gold dust, $1,000 in cash, and $150,000 in U.S. bonds.

The crew reported that three Americans had robbed them. The Pinkerton Detective Agency, known for hunting outlaws, became involved. A large reward was offered for Miner's capture. Yet Miner eluded them — at least until he robbed another train in 1906.

eluded: *avoided; escaped*

Take Note

Bill Miner takes the #8 spot. Like Black Bart, he only stole from banks and big companies and was generally liked by the public. Yet he was more dangerous than Black Bart because he carried a loaded gun and used dynamite. He also never seemed to learn his lesson, returning to crime after each jail term!

• Do some research. Find out more about Bill Miner and his crimes. How many robberies did he commit?

ALL IMAGES–ISTOCKPHOTO AND SHUTTERSTOCK

2   1

EMMETT

GRAT

ROBERT

Framed images of the Dalton brothers — Emmett, Grat, and Robert Dalton went to church on Sundays when they were in Tulsa. The wife of the church minister once said, "They sang in my husband's church on Sundays and ravaged the country during the week."

BROTHERS

EMMETT, GRAT, AND ROBERT–THE GRANGER COLLECTION, NEW YORK; ALL OTHER IMAGES–SHUTTERSTOCK

REAL NAME: Gratton (Grat), Emmett, Robert (Bob), and Bill Dalton

ALSO KNOWN AS: The Dalton Gang

ERA: 1890 to 1892

BEST KNOWN FOR: Bank and train robbing, with some horse stealing thrown in for good measure

BILL

Could it be in their blood? In 1890, four brothers from the Dalton family formed a gang with some cowboy buddies and began a crime spree that lasted for two years. The Daltons were first cousins of the famous outlaws, the Younger brothers. On top of that, they were distantly related to Jesse James. No doubt the Dalton boys grew up hearing stories of their law-breaking relatives.

Strangely, the Daltons started out on the right side of the law. Their oldest brother, Frank Dalton, was a deputy marshal who was killed in 1887 while trying to catch a crook. Gratton (Grat) and Robert (Bob) Dalton became deputy marshals, too. They were soon caught breaking the law instead of enforcing it — Grat for horse stealing and Bob for bootlegging. They went on the run, formed a gang, and were soon joined by two more Dalton brothers — Emmett and Bill. In just two years, the Dalton Brothers got into enough trouble to make them infamous and end up on our list of outrageous outlaws!

infamous: *having a very bad reputation*

THE DALTON BROTHERS

BACKGROUND

Grat, Emmett, Bob, and Bill Dalton came from a family of 15 children. Their parents were Lewis and Adeline Dalton. Many of the Dalton children were born in Missouri. Eventually, the family moved to Oklahoma's Indian Territory, a lawless area filled with raiders and gangs. At some point, Lewis Dalton abandoned his family. In 1889, Adeline Dalton and her children moved to a town near Kingfisher, Oklahoma.

MOST OUTRAGEOUS CRIMES

The Dalton brothers' last train robbery occurred in 1892, at the train station in Adair, Oklahoma. Although the train was filled with marshals for extra security, the Daltons managed to sneak onboard and steal some money. The marshals spotted them as they were leaving the train. A gun battle followed in which one bystander was killed and another wounded. Somehow the bandits got away unharmed.

The Dalton brothers' most famous heist was the one that ended their career. Bob decided to hit two banks at the same time — a feat he claimed Jesse James never managed. On October 5, 1892, six members of the Dalton Gang rode into Coffeyville, Kansas, to pull off the double robbery. Unknown to them, they were recognized. The locals quickly banded together and met the gang with a hail of bullets as they left a bank.

heist: *robbery*

IN THE END

Bob and Grat Dalton were killed in the gunfight that followed their double bank robbery in 1892. Emmett was wounded, but he recovered and was sent to jail for 14 years. Bill Dalton wasn't part of the double robbery — but he was still wanted for other crimes. In 1894, he was killed by a posse outside his home.

Quick Fact

After serving his time in prison, Emmett moved to California and became a real estate agent, author, and actor. He died in 1937.

The Condon & Co. Bank in Coffeyville, Kansas, where two of the Dalton brothers were killed

The Expert Says...

"The Dalton brothers proved to be able lawmen because they had nerves of steel and they could shoot fast and straight. Unfortunately, they tended to break the law as much as they protected it."

— *Legends of the Wild West* authors Crutchfield, O'Neal, and Walker on the Dalton brothers' law career

Outlaws Gunned Down!

This article describes how members of the Dalton Gang were killed during their attempt to rob two banks.

Shattered windows and pocked walls attest to the fatal firepower directed at the bandits.

An extract from *Galveston Daily News*, October 6, 1892

Coffeyville, Kansas — The Dalton Gang has been exterminated — wiped off the face of the earth. They were today shot down, but not until four citizens of this place yielded up their lives. ... Six of the gang rode into town this morning and robbed two banks. The raid became known to the officers of the law, and when the bandits attempted to escape they were attacked by the marshal's posse. In the battle which ensued, four of the desperadoes were killed outright, and one so fatally wounded that he has since died. The other escaped but is being hotly pursued.

It was rumored a month ago that the Dalton Gang contemplated an immediate raid upon the banks of the city. Arrangements were made to give them a warm reception, and for over a week a patrol was maintained night and day to give warning of the gang's approach. The raid did not take place ... . Then came the report ... that United States officers had had a battle with the bandits and three bandits had been killed. This report is believed here to have been circulated by the Daltons themselves, their intention being to ... lull the people of the town into a sense of security. The people, however, were not so easily deceived ...

yielded: *gave up*
ensued: *followed*
desperadoes: *bold and violent criminals*
reception: *welcome*

Take Note

The Dalton brothers take the #7 spot. They killed innocent bystanders and law officials during their crimes. However, they are not ranked higher because their criminal careers were cut short by their own arrogance — in trying to pull off the first ever double bank robbery.
- The Dalton brothers' double robbery attempt failed because of the vigilance of the town's citizens. Think of some ways in which people can get together to prevent crime in their neighborhoods.

5   4   3   2   1

Butch Cassidy (left seated), the Sundance Kid (middle seated), and the rest of the Wild Bunch posed for this picture in 1900. It's said that they sent it to the Pinkerton Detective Agency to taunt the detectives who were hunting them.

WILD BUNCH–PHOTO BY JOHN SWARTZ/AMERICAN STOCK/GETTY IMAGES

DY

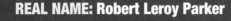

REAL NAME: Robert Leroy Parker

ALSO KNOWN AS: George Cassidy, James "Santiago" Maxwell, and William T. Phillips

ERA: 1889 to 1908

BEST KNOWN FOR: Leading the Wild Bunch, a gang of criminals who stole cattle and robbed trains and banks

Butch Cassidy was the leader of the Wild Bunch, one of the biggest and last outlaw gangs to rule the Wild West. Although best known for their daring bank and train robberies, the members of the Wild Bunch were also famous for their clever escapes. After a crime, they usually had fresh horses ready in prearranged spots along their escape route. That way they could ride for hours without stopping. The crew also had a few notorious hiding spots in the canyons of southeastern Utah. One of these was known as the Robbers' Roost.

The gang's crimes enraged a number of state governors. They issued a $1,000 reward for Butch Cassidy's head, and the heat was on! After a failed attempt at getting a pardon for past offenses, Cassidy and his sidekick, the Sundance Kid, decided they had better leave the country. They boarded a ship and set sail for South America. They bought a ranch and settled down in Argentina — until they got bored and turned to crime again. Sound like a movie? You bet! And there's more to the story...

notorious: *unfavorably known*
pardon: *legal forgiveness*

A famous movie called *Butch Cassidy and the Sundance Kid*, starring two of Hollywood's best known actors, Robert Redford and Paul Newman, came out in 1969. Find a DVD of the movie and watch it. How closely does the movie stick to facts?

BUTCH CASSIDY

BACKGROUND

Robert Leroy Parker was born in Utah on April 13, 1866. He was the eldest of 13 children. His parents, Maximillian Parker and Ann Campbell Gillies, were ranchers. Parker left home in his early teens and became friends with rancher Mike Cassidy. Mike is said to have introduced Parker to the outlaw life.

Quick Fact

Parker started using the last name "Cassidy" in honor of his mentor, Mike Cassidy. He likely gained the nickname "Butch" during the brief time he worked as a ranch butcher.

MOST OUTRAGEOUS CRIMES

Butch Cassidy was involved in so many crimes, it's hard to pick just one! But here's one example: In 1897, two strangers arrived in Castle Gate, Utah, looking for jobs. Of course, they were really Cassidy and another gang member casing the area. On April 21, the outlaws ambushed some guards carrying a coal company payroll worth $7,000. Cassidy and his pal escaped by outriding the law using horses that they had hidden along their escape route.

casing: *inspecting; examining*

IN THE END

Other than spending a short time in jail for horse stealing, Cassidy was never arrested for his crimes. In 1901, he and the Sundance Kid moved to Argentina and bought a ranch. They sold it when the law began to catch up with them. After that, the two lived a life of crime in South America. No one knows for sure when they died, but some believe it was November 6, 1908. On that night, a Bolivian posse surrounded two American bandits in a house. The two men were later found dead. Were those bandits Butch Cassidy and the Sundance Kid? The men were buried in unmarked graves, so no one knows for sure.

Quick Fact

Butch Cassidy's sister Lula wrote a biography about her brother. According to Lula, her brother actually died in Washington State in 1937, not in Bolivia.

? Do you think living life "on the run" all the time would be exciting or hard? Explain.

The Expert Says...

" Operating around the turn of the century, Cassidy and his partners put together the longest sequence of successful bank and train robberies in the history of the American West. "

— John D. Barton, *Utah History Encyclopedia*

10

6

What really happened to Butch Cassidy?

Butch Cassidy

Did Butch Cassidy really die in Bolivia in 1908? Many suspect that he didn't. They think he moved to Spokane, Washington, and began using the name William T. Phillips. This man claimed to have been a "childhood friend" of Butch Cassidy, had several of Butch Cassidy's belongings, and wrote a book about Cassidy. Check out an excerpt from Phillips' book.

Many descriptions have been written of Butch Cassidy by many various men. ... It has been my pleasure to have known Butch Cassidy since his early boyhood and I am happy to say I have never known a more courageous and kinder-hearted man in my lifetime. His reputation for ... integrity in all his dealing aside from holdups is unquestioned. ...

Cassidy did not rob for ... gain ... . He had as he thought every good reason for his first holdup, and after the first, there was no place to stop.

I cannot help but feel that he was entirely a victim of circumstance and that in a way he was goaded on to become the most dreaded, the most hunted ... outlaw that either North or South America have had to contend with as yet ...

goaded: urged

 If William Phillips was indeed Butch Cassidy, he is describing himself in this text. Why might he write an autobiography?

Take Note

Butch Cassidy takes the #6 spot. He was a gun-wielding bank robber who spent his life as a career criminal. Unlike the Dalton Gang, which had a short criminal career, Butch Cassidy spent most of his life living on the wild side. Although it's said he never killed anyone, he did use his gun during robberies. His notoriety and the mystery surrounding his death have endured to this day.

- Do you think Butch Cassidy slipped away to Washington and lived under a new name, as many people believed? Give reasons for your answer.

5   4   3   2   1

5 MA BARKER AND THE

Ma Barker and her close friend, Arthur W. Dunlop

BARKER–KARPIS GANG

REAL NAME: Ma Barker's real name was Arizona (Clark) Barker. Her sons' names were Herman, Lloyd, Arthur, and Fred. They later met up with Alvin Karpis (whose birth name was Alvin Karpowicz).

ALSO KNOWN AS: "Ma" Barker was also known as "Kate" Barker. Arthur Barker's nickname was "Doc" and Alvin Karpis's nickname was "Old Creepy."

ERA: 1920s and especially 1931–35

BEST KNOWN FOR: Sticking together as family while committing bank robberies, kidnappings, and murder

It's hard to believe that someone known as "Ma" was a criminal or the mother of four of the most ruthless criminals ever. Ma's boys (Herman, Lloyd, Arthur, and Fred) started off as petty criminals. But when Fred Barker met Alvin Karpis in jail and convinced him to join their gang in 1931, they hit the big time.

Karpis had a photographic memory and strong organizational skills. He was also ruthless. Although some folks might argue that Ma was the mastermind behind the Barker–Karpis gang, most people agree it was really Karpis. He helped the gang to plan huge heists — including one that netted them $250,000.

In 1932, the Barker–Karpis gang robbed 11 banks. They did not hesitate to kill anyone who got in their way. They also hijacked mail deliveries and kidnapped victims for ransom. They were one of the most fearsome criminal gangs of the 1930s.

petty: *of little importance or value*

MA BARKER AND THE BARKER-KARPIS GANG

BACKGROUND

Ma Barker was born Arizona Clark in 1872 in Springfield, Missouri. She married farm laborer George Barker and had four sons. The family was very poor. In 1927, "Kate," or "Ma," as she was known to her boys, left her husband. She lived the rest of her life on the run with her sons.

Alvin Karpis, who later joined the Barker gang, was born in Montreal, Canada, in 1907 and raised in Topeka, Kansas. He started his life of crime at age 10 by running errands for other petty criminals.

MOST OUTRAGEOUS CRIMES

In 1934, the gang kidnapped Minnesota banker Edward Bremer Jr. They released him in exchange for a $200,000 ransom. Unfortunately for the gang, Bremer's father was a friend of President Franklin Roosevelt. After the kidnapping, President Roosevelt put more pressure on the FBI to catch the gang.

Quick Fact
Not a bad haul! The Barkers got as much as $3 million from all their criminal activities.

IN THE END

In 1927, Herman Barker was found dead by the police. In 1935, Arthur Barker was arrested in Chicago. A short time later, the FBI found Ma and Fred Barker's hideout in Lake Weir, Florida. Both Barkers were killed in a gun battle some say lasted at least four hours. Alvin Karpis was arrested a year later. Lloyd Barker, who had been in prison since 1932, was killed by his wife in 1949 after he was paroled.

Quick Fact
Arthur Barker was killed in 1939 while trying to escape from the prison on Alcatraz Island, California.

Ma and Fred Barker were killed at their Florida hideout after a long gun battle with the FBI.

Was She or Wasn't She?

In the 1930s, most people believed that "Ma" was the real head of the Barker–Karpis gang. Today, some experts suggest the FBI might have started this story to cover up the fact that they killed an "innocent" old woman (Ma) in their shootout with Fred Barker. Read these two accounts about Ma Barker and see where you weigh in on the debate.

"The most ridiculous story in the annals of crime is that Ma Barker was the mastermind behind (our) gang … . She wasn't a leader of criminals or even a criminal herself. There is not one police photograph of her or set of fingerprints taken while she was alive … . She knew we were criminals, but … when we traveled together, we moved as a mother and her sons …"

— Alvin Karpis in his book with Bill Trent, called *The Alvin Karpis Story*

Toronto Star, January 17, 1935

MACHINE-GUNNING "MA" HELD BRAINS OF KARPIS GANG

… Fred [Barker] and [his] mother were slain yesterday during a five-hour machine-gun fight in Florida with federal operatives. The 55-year-old "Ma" Barker, whose hair was dyed a jet black, died with a machine-gun still hot in her hands. With "Ma" out of the way, federal officers believe capture of her other son and Karpis is imminent. The agents said the gang never would have survived as long as it did, had it not been for "Ma's" brains …

---

imminent: *about to happen soon*

The Expert Says…

" Ma Barker and her sons, and Alvin Karpis and his cronies, were the toughest gang of hoodlums the FBI ever has been called upon to eliminate. … Looking over the record of these criminals, I was repeatedly impressed by [their] cruelty … "

— FBI Director J. Edgar Hoover, quoted in the book *The FBI In Action* by Ken Jones (1957)

Take Note

A mother-and-son gang is pretty outrageous. But the real reason these guys are #5 on our list is that they robbed, killed, and kidnapped for many years. The members of the Barker–Karpis gang were much more ruthless than Butch Cassidy and the other outlaws on our list so far.

• Who do you think was the real leader of this gang — Ma Barker or Alvin Karpis? Explain.

5   4   3   2   1

The first man to die at Billy's hands was Frank Cahill. He was a blacksmith at the army post where Billy worked when he was only 17. Apparently, Billy killed Frank because he was being bullied by him.

REAL NAME: Henry McCarty

ALSO KNOWN AS: William H. Bonney and "Billy the Kid"

ERA: 1875 to 1881

BEST KNOWN FOR: Murder, theft, gambling, and escaping from law officials

For someone who only lived to be 21, Billy the Kid got himself in a whole heap of trouble. His first brush with the law occurred when he was 15. At age 17, he killed his first man. By the time he died, this gunslinger had taken the lives of at least eight other men and probably more.

Billy the Kid spent much of his short life stealing, gambling, and killing. This got him arrested several times — but each time he managed to escape. Besides slipping out of handcuffs many times, Billy escaped a jailhouse by climbing up the chimney. He also broke out of a courthouse while under armed guard.

Despite his violent lifestyle, Billy the Kid wasn't widely feared while he was alive. However, after Billy was killed by Sheriff Garrett, the sheriff wrote a book about him. The biography was filled with tall tales that helped make Billy the Kid into a legend.

 Why do you think the man who killed Billy the Kid would tell tales about the outlaw?

BILLY THE KID

BACKGROUND

The details of Billy the Kid's early life are unclear. But it's thought he was born as Henry McCarty in 1859 in New York City. Billy was about 10 when his father died. In 1873, his mother remarried. The family spent time in Silver City, New Mexico, before moving to Kansas. After his mother died from tuberculosis in 1874, Billy and his half-brother were raised by her husband.

> **?** Compare Billy to another outlaw in the book. What is different in the way each of them turned to crime?

MOST OUTRAGEOUS CRIMES

When he was 18, Billy took a job on a ranch in Lincoln County, New Mexico. His boss was involved in a local feud between long-time merchants in the area (called the "House") and newer ranchers. Billy witnessed "House" members murder his boss. So Billy and a few ranch hands formed a group to seek revenge. As part of this group, Billy was involved in the shooting of the local sheriff. Billy became a wanted man because a law officer had been killed.

---

tuberculosis: *infectious disease of the lungs*

IN THE END

Patrick Garrett began tracking Billy for the murder of the sheriff in Lincoln County. Sheriff Garrett caught Billy once, but he managed to escape. Then in July 1881, Garrett tracked Billy to a friend's house and waited for him. It was dark when Billy entered the house, so he asked in Spanish, "Who is it? Who is it?" Sheriff Garrett recognized Billy's voice and fired twice. The first bullet hit Billy and killed him.

The Expert Says...

" Four months into the Lincoln County War, Billy Boney had become an accomplished fighter, rash at times, but confident in his abilities. … He had also grown callous toward human life and stood ready to kill … by means fair or foul, when the cause seemed to require it. "

— Author Robert Marshall Utley in his book, *Billy the Kid: A Short and Violent Life*

Quick Fact

Pals in life, pals in death … Billy the Kid was buried in a military cemetery between two of his fallen outlaw friends. A single tombstone was later erected over the graves with their names and the word "Pals" carved into it.

BILLY'S GREAT ESCAPE

Billy the Kid was killed by Patrick Garrett in 1881 — but that was not their first run-in. Garrett and two deputies also managed to capture Billy in 1880 …

A BIG HAUL!

An article from *Las Vegas Daily Optic*, December 27, 1880

… Our readers are familiar with … Billy Kid, and the repeated and unsuccessful attempts to capture [him and his men]. They have roamed over the country at will, placing no value upon human life, and [stealing from] ranchmen and travelers … Posses of men have been in hot pursuit of them for weeks, but they succeeded in eluding their pursuers every time. However, the right boys started out … and were successful in bagging their game.

Yesterday afternoon the town was into a fever of excitement by an announcement that the "Kid" and other members of his gang of outlaws had been captured …

Sheriff Garrett

Billy the Kid had been captured — but it didn't last long! Since Billy was sentenced to hang, Garrett arranged for Billy to be kept in a courthouse under armed guard until his execution. However, he decided not to wait around. Billy managed to get a gun and shoot the two deputies who were guarding him. He did not see Sheriff Garrett again until the night Garrett killed him.

Take Note

Billy the Kid takes the #4 spot. His murdering spree started when he was 17. He killed at least nine people and possibly as many as 21. He was supposedly short-tempered and murdered some of his victims over small arguments. If he had lived longer, his list of victims would have likely grown. On top of this, Billy's ability to escape from custody made him even more of an outrageous outlaw.

• Billy the Kid was a thief and a ruthless murderer, yet he has been immortalized in books and movies. Do you think criminals should be remembered in this way? Explain.

4   3   2   1

John Dillinger is photographed here with fellow gang members.

GER

REAL NAME: John Herbert Dillinger

ALSO KNOWN AS: Jackrabbit, because of his easy leaps over counters during bank heists

ERA: 1924 to 1934

BEST KNOWN FOR: Robbing banks and escaping from jail

JOHN DILLINGER–© BETTMANN/CORBIS

What does someone have to do to be named the FBI's Public Enemy Number One? In John Dillinger's case he led two gangs, killed at least 10 people, escaped from two jails, stole weapons from police arsenals, and helped plan one of the largest jailbreaks in Indiana history. He also robbed banks — a lot of them.

In the 1930s, when John Dillinger was robbing banks, outlaws were often known as gangsters. Like the outlaws of the Wild West, many of these men captured the public's interest. After all, the early 1930s was the time of the Great Depression when many people were starving. People who took what they wanted were sometimes admired. This was especially true in Dillinger's case. He was handsome and charming — and taking what he wanted was exactly what Dillinger did best.

Dillinger and his gangs netted about $300,000 from bank robberies — a fortune during the Depression! But Dillinger was also a cold-blooded killer. His crimes eventually caught the attention of the FBI and led to his death. Or did it ...?

 Can you think of any modern-day criminals who are seen in a positive way by the public?

JOHN DILLINGER

BACKGROUND

John Dillinger was born in Indianapolis, Indiana, in 1903. His father was a grocer. His mother died when Dillinger was just three. A troubled youth, Dillinger did not stay in school long. In 1923, he joined the navy, but deserted soon after. In 1924, Dillinger started his life of crime when he and his pal mugged a local merchant. He was caught and sent to jail for almost nine years. While in jail, Dillinger made friends with some hard-core criminals and learned their ways. One of the first things Dillinger did when he was paroled was rob a bank.

Quick Fact

When John Dillinger was 21, he married 16-year-old Beryl Hovius from his hometown. The marriage didn't last long.

? Why do you think so many people were interested in seeing the dead body of John Dillinger?

Federal agents caught up with the elusive John Dillinger and killed him as he was leaving the Biograph Theater in Chicago.

MOST OUTRAGEOUS CRIMES

Dillinger was known for robbing banks and escaping from jail. After his first bank robbery, Dillinger was arrested and sent to prison. His gang pals broke him out. Several months and many crimes later, Dillinger was recaptured and sent to an "escape proof" jail in Indiana. But it couldn't hold him either. On March 3, 1934, Dillinger pulled a "gun" — supposedly one carved out of wood and covered with black shoe polish — on the guards. Then he escaped in the sheriff's brand-new car.

In April 1934, the FBI was tipped off about the whereabouts of Dillinger. He was hiding with his gang in a summer resort called Little Bohemia in northern Wisconsin. The FBI surrounded the resort and kept watch. One night, when the FBI saw three people in a car about to leave the resort, they opened fire. It was a horrible mistake — the passengers in the car were innocent victims. The Dillinger gang escaped after killing an FBI agent.

IN THE END

On July 22, 1934, Dillinger said he'd take his girlfriend and her pal, Anna Sage, to see a film in Chicago. Anna was from Romania and was facing deportation charges. She called the FBI to tell them where Dillinger would be in exchange for cash and the chance to remain in the U.S. The FBI surrounded the theater and killed Dillinger on his way out.

The Expert Says...

" ... Hordes of the curious began arriving that night ... until the doors of this house of the dead were finally closed at midnight ... There on the cold slab of the morgue lay the outlaw's body ... They passed before him — the men gaping with open mouths, the women shuddering and covering their eyes, or emitting short hysterical screams. "

— George Russell Girardin, an advertising executive, describing the crowds of almost 15,000 people who went to see John Dillinger's body

THE "DEATH" OF DILLINGER

Was Dillinger really killed in front of the Chicago theater on July 22, 1934? Some people think not. Famous crime writer Jay Robert Nash believes that the man the FBI actually killed was a criminal named Jimmy Lawrence who looked like Dillinger. Was John's death really just an FBI cover-up? Whether it was or not, the FBI is sticking to its story. Here is part of their official report:

From the FBI file written by Inspector Samuel P. Cowley of the FBI's Chicago Office

July 24, 1934

Re: John Herbert Dillinger,

… About ten-thirty o'clock on the night of July 22, 1934, Dillinger, accompanied by two women companions, was observed emerging from the Biograph Theater … . Special Agent in Charge, M.H. Purvis, gave the pre-arranged signal of lighting a cigar. Agents immediately began to close in slowly toward Dillinger from all sides.

Dillinger … glanced over his shoulder at Agents and started to run, grabbing for his gun … . Agent C.B. Winstead fired one shot. This was immediately followed by … [shots from other agents].

Dillinger fell face downward near an alley. A … pistol was in his hand when he fell. No shots were fired from Dillinger's pistol. An extra clip for his pistol was found in his pocket.

Dillinger was removed to the Hospital at 10:55 P.M. where he was pronounced dead. … the body of Dillinger was taken to the County Morgue.

Very truly yours,
S.P. Cowley
Special Agent

Quick Fact

It's said that when Dillinger's father came to identify his son's body at the morgue, he cried out, "That's not my boy!" Yet his sister did identify the body as her brother's. Hmmm…

Take Note

John Dillinger takes the #3 spot. Intelligent and highly organized, he was able to work out complicated plans, including breaking out of escape-proof jails. A violent and ruthless criminal, he killed many people and looted many banks.

• Despite the FBI report describing Dillinger's death, some people still believe that the wrong man was killed. There are many urban legends about the "non-deaths" of famous people. Why do you think such stories endure?

5   4   **3**   2   1

Jesse James has been the subject of many books and movies. The latest movie, starring Brad Pitt as Jesse James, was filmed in 2007.

REAL NAME: Jesse Woodson James

ALSO KNOWN AS: Thomas Howard

ERA: 1866 to 1882

BEST KNOWN FOR: Robbing banks and trains

What is it about Jesse James? He was famous during the latter part of his life and became a legend after his death. There are movies, books, and songs about him. He was a robber and murderer, yet he's captured the public's imagination.

During his lifetime, James liked to portray himself as a gunslinging Robin Hood. At age 17, he joined his brother Frank as a guerrilla, or "bushwhacker," for the Confederates. Other bushwhackers sided with the Union. They all operated more like bandits than soldiers. They used the Civil War as an excuse for criminal activity such as robbery, arson, and even murder.

When the war ended, the James brothers were not content to return to regular life. They started robbing banks. Because the brothers were linked to the Confederate side of the war, many Southerners supported them. Eventually, the James brothers joined another group, the Younger brothers, to form the James–Younger gang. This gang robbed over 20 banks, held up stagecoaches and trains, and killed at least 10 people. Although James did rob from the "rich" — there isn't any evidence that he gave his money to the "poor." However, he did sometimes pay off townspeople to hide him. That added to his Robin Hood reputation, which still survives today!

 Robin Hood was an outlaw in medieval England who robbed from the rich to give to the poor. Do you think Jesse James was a Robin Hood type of outlaw? Explain.

JESSE JAMES

BACKGROUND

Jesse James was born in 1847 in Clay County, Missouri, to Robert and Zerelda James. James had a younger sister, Susan, and an older brother, Frank. (Frank later became one of his partners in crime.) When James was three, his father died of cholera. His mother remarried and had four more children. The family lived on a tobacco farm.

Quick Fact

In 1875, detectives from the Pinkerton Detective Agency raided the James's family farm. They used a firebomb that killed Jesse James's half-brother and wounded his mother. This bungled operation received national coverage and raised public sympathy for James.

MOST OUTRAGEOUS CRIMES

James's most daring heist turned out to be a dud. In 1876, he and the James–Younger gang tried to rob a bank in Northfield, Minnesota. Unlike their past targets, this bank was in Union territory where the public had no sympathy for ex-Confederate outlaws. Their trouble started as soon as they entered the bank. The cashier tricked them by saying he couldn't open the safe because it was on a time lock. The outlaws murdered him and left the bank empty-handed. Outside, they were met by armed townspeople. A shoot-out ensued. Some members were killed and others barely escaped.

cholera: *disease that causes stomach cramps, vomiting, and diarrhea*

Quick Fact

After the failed Minnesota bank robbery, a massive manhunt caught all the members of the James–Younger gang. Jesse and Frank James managed to escape.

IN THE END

After the demise of their gang, James and Frank Younger moved to Tennessee and lived under fake names. Younger settled down, but James eventually started up a new gang. Two of the new gang members, Bob and Charley Ford, lived with James. Wanting a reward, Bob secretly began working with the Missouri governor to capture James. On April 3, 1882, the Ford brothers saw their chance. When James removed his guns to straighten a picture on the wall, the Ford brothers drew their guns. Bob shot James in the back of the head and killed him.

The Expert Says...

"If Jesse James had been hunted down as any other criminal and killed while trying to escape, or in resisting arrest, not a word would have been said to the contrary … but here the law itself becomes a murderer. It borrows money to pay and reward murderers … this so-called law is an outlaw; and these so called executioners of the law are outlaws."

— John Edwards, former editor of the *Kansas City Times*

10   **9**   **8**   **7**   **6**

The Legend Lives On

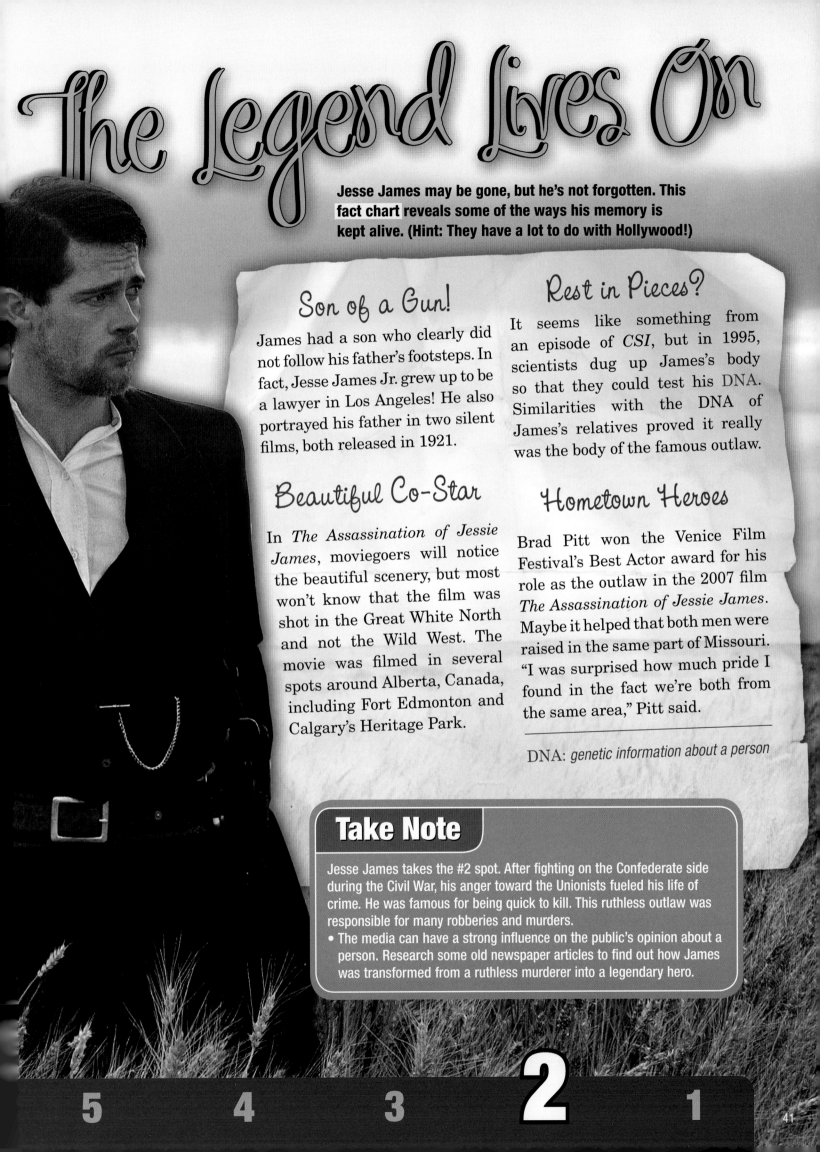

Jesse James may be gone, but he's not forgotten. This fact chart reveals some of the ways his memory is kept alive. (Hint: They have a lot to do with Hollywood!)

Son of a Gun!

James had a son who clearly did not follow his father's footsteps. In fact, Jesse James Jr. grew up to be a lawyer in Los Angeles! He also portrayed his father in two silent films, both released in 1921.

Beautiful Co-Star

In *The Assassination of Jessie James*, moviegoers will notice the beautiful scenery, but most won't know that the film was shot in the Great White North and not the Wild West. The movie was filmed in several spots around Alberta, Canada, including Fort Edmonton and Calgary's Heritage Park.

Rest in Pieces?

It seems like something from an episode of *CSI*, but in 1995, scientists dug up James's body so that they could test his DNA. Similarities with the DNA of James's relatives proved it really was the body of the famous outlaw.

Hometown Heroes

Brad Pitt won the Venice Film Festival's Best Actor award for his role as the outlaw in the 2007 film *The Assassination of Jessie James*. Maybe it helped that both men were raised in the same part of Missouri. "I was surprised how much pride I found in the fact we're both from the same area," Pitt said.

DNA: *genetic information about a person*

Take Note

Jesse James takes the #2 spot. After fighting on the Confederate side during the Civil War, his anger toward the Unionists fueled his life of crime. He was famous for being quick to kill. This ruthless outlaw was responsible for many robberies and murders.

• The media can have a strong influence on the public's opinion about a person. Research some old newspaper articles to find out how James was transformed from a ruthless murderer into a legendary hero.

5   4   3   2   1

BONNIE AND

The notorious Bonnie Parker and Clyde Barrow

CLYDE

REAL NAME: Bonnie Elizabeth Parker and Clyde Chestnut Barrow

ALSO KNOWN AS: "Suicide Sal" (Parker) and the "Texas Rattlesnake" (Barrow)

ERA: Barrow started breaking the law in 1927. Parker joined him in 1930 and they continued until their deaths in 1934.

BEST KNOWN FOR: Robbing, murdering, and kidnapping people while they lived on the run

Bonnie Parker and Clyde Barrow were partners in life and in crime. The pair met at a friend's house in the early 1920s. It seemed to be love at first sight, and they became inseparable. The couple were to become the most legendary criminals ever hunted in America.

Bonnie Parker and Clyde Barrow ran with the Barrow Gang, which included Clyde's brother, Buck, and Buck's wife, Blanche. The gang robbed small stores, gas stations, and banks; got into deadly gun battles with the authorities; and were responsible for the deaths of nine law enforcement officers and four civilians. Though Parker participated in these crimes, it's thought she never actually fired a gun.

The gang always seemed to narrowly escape capture by the law. All over the country, people talked and wrote about their escapades. This all took place during the Great Depression. Many people were without hope and blamed the bad times on the government and corporate America. To these people, Bonnie Parker and Clyde Barrow were heroes beating the system. The public cheered them on — most of the time.

? Do you think the fact that they were a couple made Bonnie and Clyde more appealing to the public? Explain.

43

BONNIE AND CLYDE

BACKGROUND

Bonnie Parker was born in Texas in 1908, and Clyde Barrow was born a year later. Both grew up in poverty. Parker was a clever student, but got married at 16 to a man who was soon imprisoned for burglary. They separated, but never divorced. Barrow was a high-school dropout. He began robbing grocery stores and gas stations. Shortly after meeting Parker in 1930, he was sent to jail. He managed to escape when Parker smuggled him a gun, but he was soon recaptured. After Barrow was paroled in 1932, he returned to crime.

MOST OUTRAGEOUS CRIMES

Barrow felt he was mistreated while in jail. He vowed to get revenge against the Texas Department of Corrections. In 1934, he did. He and Parker helped break out five criminals from the Eastham State Prison Farm. This caused the Department of Corrections a lot of embarrassment.

IN THE END

Seeking revenge, the Texas Department of Corrections hired a former Texas Ranger to hunt down Bonnie and Clyde. The Ranger was helped by the father of a gang member charged with murder. He wanted his son to avoid the death penalty so he gave the police information that helped them find the couple. On May 23, 1934, the Ranger and other law officers waited as the couple drove a stolen car down a small road in Louisiana. They greeted the couple with over 100 rounds of ammunition. Bonnie Parker and Clyde Barrow were both killed.

? The law officers were later criticized because they didn't offer the outlaws a chance to surrender before shooting them. Do you think their actions were justified? Why or why not?

Quick Fact

People can do strange things — some became scavengers when the couple was gunned down. They took bits of the couple's bloody clothing and locks of their hair. A Nevada casino later paid thousands of dollars for the bullet-riddled shirt worn by Clyde Barrow when he was ambushed.

The car Bonnie Parker and Clyde Barrow were killed in was riddled with at least 70 bullets.

9 8 7 6

LAW OFFICER'S WIDOW UPSET OVER FAME OF BONNIE AND CLYDE

An article from the *Fort Worth Star-Telegram*
By Bud Kennedy, June 1, 1996

One woman in North Texas has heard plenty about new books, TV shows, or museum exhibits on 1930s outlaws Clyde Barrow and Bonnie Parker.

"What is everybody thinking?" Doris Edwards asked. "My husband was killed by Bonnie and Clyde.

"We get to hear Clyde's little sister call him 'a good boy' on talk shows. We even see her soaking up attention at book signings …"

But there are no book signings for the widow of a slain Texas state trooper, and not many calls to her home in the North Texas countryside.

"It's like we don't even count," she said, slowly retelling the news of Easter Sunday morning April 1, 1934, when her young husband and a rookie trooper were killed on Dove Road in Grapevine.

E. B. Wheeler

E. B. Wheeler was helping train H. D. Murphy when they rode up on motorcycles to check a parked car. Inside were Bonnie and Clyde. In an instant, Wheeler and Murphy became Texas's first troopers killed on duty. They were two of nine officers murdered by the outlaws …

"… Glorifying these killers insults all of us."

Wheeler and Murphy are remembered only in highway patrol archives.

The Expert Says…

"It has to do with the fact that here's a young boy and a young girl who — at the time, in the Depression — went against the system … And they were a young couple who were so much in love that they were going to stay together, even if it meant dying. I think in our romantic notion of it, that's appealing to the general public.

— John Phillips, author of *Running with Bonnie and Clyde*, during a CNN interview

Take Note

Why are Bonnie and Clyde in the top spot? We think they're more vicious than Jesse James. They seemed to have a complete disregard for human life. It appears that the only thing they cared about was each other. They didn't always cash in on big hauls, nor did they seem to plan their crimes. They just shot at anyone who stood in their way. This made them illogical, willing to take greater risks, and very, very dangerous.
- Very often, as this newspaper article shows, the criminals are remembered and their victims are forgotten. Why do you think this is so, and how can the situation be changed?

5   4   3   2   **1**

Here are the criteria we used in ranking the 10 most outrageous outlaws.

The outlaw:
- Committed dangerous crimes
- Behaved ruthlessly and unpredictably
- Captured the public's imagination
- Earned a great deal of media attention
- Had a lengthy criminal career
- Avoided capture or made a dramatic escape
- Had a wild reputation
- Inspired many books, movies, and TV shows

EMMETT

GRAT

ROBERT

BILL

What Do You Think?

1. Do you agree with our ranking? If you don't, try ranking these outlaws yourself. Justify your ranking with data from your own research and reasoning. You may refer to our criteria, or you may want to draw up your own list of criteria.

2. Here are three other outlaws that we considered but in the end did not include in our top 10 list: Cherokee Bill, Pearl Heart, and Rattlesnake Dick.
   • Find out more about these outlaws. Do you think they should have made our list? Give reasons for your response.
   • Are there other outrageous outlaws that you think should have made our list? Explain your choices.

Index